$12.89

DATE			

halloween

A CROWELL hOLiDAY BOOK

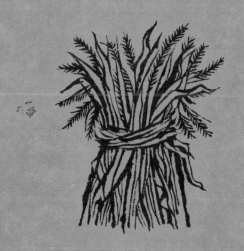

HALLOWEEN

WRITTEN AND ILLUSTRATED

BY helen Borten

thomas y. Crowell Company

new york

CROWELL HOLIDAY BOOKS

Edited by Susan Bartlett Weber

New Year's Day
Lincoln's Birthday
St. Valentine's Day
Washington's Birthday
Purim
St. Patrick's Day
Passover
Easter
Arbor Day
May Day
Mother's Day
Flag Day
The Fourth of July

Labor Day
The Jewish New Year
Columbus Day
United Nations Day
Halloween
Election Day
Thanksgiving Day
Human Rights Day
Hanukkah
Christmas
The Jewish Sabbath
Indian Festivals
Skip Around the Year

TO PETER BECAUSE
OCTOBER 31 IS HIS BIRTHDAY

October 31 is a night for make-believe witches and ghosts in pillow cases. It is for funny masks and pirate hats and devils' tails. It is for glued-on moustaches and wearing Mommy's lipstick.

October 31 is for ringing doorbells and giggling, for shouting *BOO* and guessing who. It is for apples and cookies and candy corn. October 31 is Halloween.

Long ago people really believed that ghosts walked and witches flew on Halloween. Hundreds of years before the birth of Christ the Celts, who lived in the British Isles and France, held a festival something like Halloween. It was called Samhain, which means "the end of summer."

Priests, called Druids, offered sacrifices to the sun god and the god of the dead. They thanked the sun god for the harvest which was safely stored away for the winter. They performed magic rites. Chanting their magic, they marched around a circle of giant stone pillars.

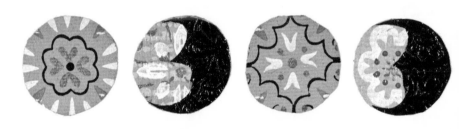

The Celts believed that during Samhain the ghosts of the dead came to earth. They lit great bonfires on the hilltops to frighten these ghosts away.

Many years later the Romans came to Britain. They also had a harvest festival, and added customs of their own to Samhain. They brought gifts of apples and nuts to their goddess Pomona.

Ever since that time apples and nuts have been a part of Halloween.

Then Christianity took the place of the Druid and Roman religions. The Christian church, in the ninth century, set aside November 1 to honor all its saints.

November 1 became known as All Hallows' or All Saints' Day. The evening before was called All Hallow's Even which means "holy evening." Later the name was shortened to Halloween.

Even though Halloween got its name from a Christian holy day, it was still celebrated with some Druid customs. Horses and oxen were sacrificed. Fairies and goblins, as well as ghosts, were supposed to visit earth.

Wise old women, called "witches,"
foretold the future. Magic words and
charms were used to keep away bad
luck.

The church tried hard to stop the practice of magic or "witchcraft." But people who worked in witchcraft banded together and made fun of the church. On Halloween they held large meetings called witches' sabbaths. They feasted, sang, and danced wildly in a ring. They promised to use their magic power to do mischief and said they were servants of the Devil.

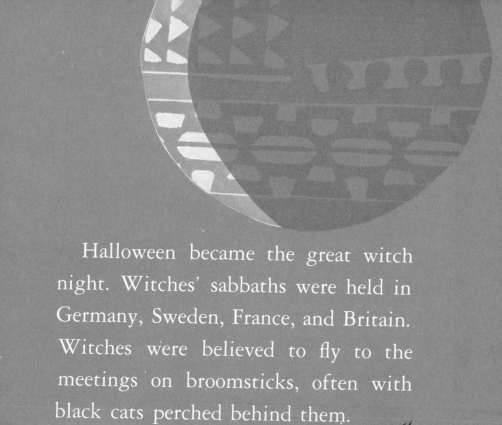

Halloween became the great witch night. Witches' sabbaths were held in Germany, Sweden, France, and Britain. Witches were believed to fly to the meetings on broomsticks, often with black cats perched behind them.

The black cats were thought to be mascots of the witches, or sometimes even witches in disguise. In Ireland black cats were thrown into Halloween fires as a warning to other witches. Other animals, such as the toad and the sow, were believed to be witches' helpers too.

People were afraid of these witches who kept company with the Devil. In Scotland, Ireland, and Scandinavia, farmers sometimes twined pitchforks with straw and set fire to them. They waved them in the air to singe the brooms of any witches who might be passing by. They made crosses out of branches and hung them on stable doors to keep their animals from harm.

It was not until hundreds of years later that people stopped believing in witches.

In Ireland and Scotland today, some of the old Druid and Roman customs can still be seen on Halloween. Country people still build bonfires on the hilltops. Some of them still wave flaming pitchforks in the air.

At parties they eat apples and nuts. They try to see into the future like the witches of old by playing fortune-telling games.

An old Halloween game played in Scotland today is "pou the stocks." Boys and girls walk hand in hand to a cabbage patch. There they shut their eyes and pull up a cabbage.

If the stalk is straight, it means they will marry someone strong and healthy. If it is shriveled or crooked, they will marry someone sickly. If earth clings to the roots, they will marry someone rich. If the roots come out clean, they will marry someone poor.

When people from Ireland and Scotland came to America they brought their Halloween customs with them. But it was not until the 1840's, after many, many Irish arrived, that Halloween was celebrated throughout the United States.

In the early days of our country October 31 was a night for bonfires and hayrides, parties and practical jokes. Great piles of fallen leaves were set aflame. Children, carrying torches, marched around the fires. Then it was time for popping corn and ducking for apples, for pulling taffy and telling ghost stories.

Mischief-makers changed house numbers and street signs. They took off gates so that cows and pigs wandered into the streets. The next morning wagons were sometimes found on barn roofs, and rocking chairs in trees.

Today on Halloween American children dress up in funny costumes and masks. They go begging and say "Trick or treat!" at each door. Neighbors fill their bags with candy, cookies, apples, and popcorn.

Begging is like an old English custom called "a souling." On All Souls' Day in England, people used to go from house to house calling, "A soulcake, a soulcake, a penny or a soulcake!" They were given little currant buns, or "soulcakes." In return they said prayers for the souls of the giver's dead relatives.

f course, Halloween is pumpkin time, too. Pumpkin faces grin at us from windows and doorsteps.

The first jack-o'-lanterns were made by the Irish. They were carved from large potatoes and turnips, for there were no pumpkins in Ireland years ago. Candles were put inside to make lanterns. An Irish legend tells how this custom began.

A man named Jack was kept out of Heaven because he was stingy. The gates of Hell were closed to him, too, because he had played jokes on the Devil. Poor Jack, carrying a lantern to light his way, was supposed to walk the earth forever.

Now on Halloween there are costume parties and carnivals and parades. There are games and good things to eat. Wherever we look we see pointed hats and flying broomsticks, spooks, skeletons, and black cats. They are made of crepe paper and paint, sugar and gingerbread, cardboard and cloth.

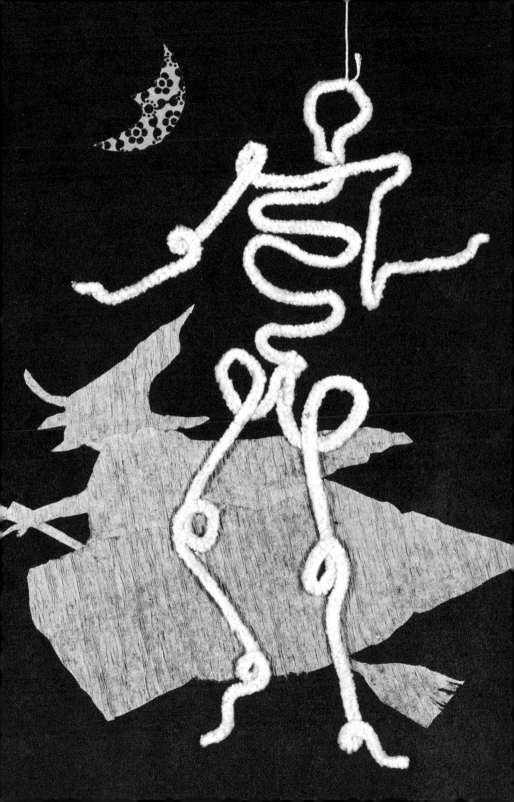

But they remind us that for two thousand years people believed that real ghosts and witches roamed the earth on Halloween.

ABOUT MRS. BORTEN

Helen Borten has illustrated a number of books for children, and she is the author and illustrator of several others.

Mrs. Borten was born in Philadelphia, Pennsylvania, and was graduated from the Philadelphia Museum College of Art. She lives with her husband and two sons, Peter and Laurence, in Lafayette Hill, Pennsylvania.